My Shopping List

Seeds for the garden,

Some food for the dog,

A rug like the one

In the catalog.

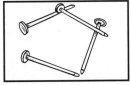

A bag full of nails,

A bottle of glue,

Two yellow ribbons

To tie on my shoe.

A book, a bracelet,

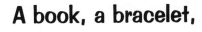

A licorice twist.

You can find them all

On my shopping list.

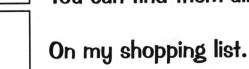

Jill Norris

A Shopping "Center"

Learning centers allow young students to explore and experiment with real-world roles. Here are suggestions for setting up a basic shopping center.

Throughout the unit you can change the props in the center to change the type of store (see page 4).

Patterns are provided on pages 6-12 for many items needed in most "stores."

Basic Shopping Center

For a basic center you will need:
- an area with a small table to serve as a counter
- a display area
- a cash register or "money box"
- shopping bags
- a spot to hang store name and advertise specials
- play money and receipts
- name tags for store employees
- pens/pencils
- price tags
- sale signs and display labels

Introducing a Center

- Talk with students about their experiences at a store like the one represented by the center. What kinds of things were sold in the store? What did the store employees do?
- Introduce the props to the children. Discuss their uses.
- Talk about the uses of different kinds of signs and how items are priced and labeled.
- Model how to write a sales receipt.
- Have students make signs for sale items.
- Read books that support the center activities. See the bibliography on the inside back cover for suggestions.

Managing Center Activities

Before students use the shopping center, develop expectations for participation.
- Determine whether there will be a time limit for center work.
- Decide how participants will be chosen. Make sure that everyone gets a chance to participate.
- Demonstrate appropriate use of the equipment in the center.
- Outline clean-up procedures.
- Have students demonstrate "on-task" behavior at the center.

Assessing Student Progress

Observe students as they work and play in the shopping center.
Use the assessment checklist on page 5 to organize your observations.
- Check specific behaviors observed.
- Note special problems.
- Use the checklist to plan lessons in areas of need.

Creating Specific Stores

Here are some suggestions for props to create different types of stores. Ask parents to supply the needed items.

Clothing Store:
clothing items to sell, accessories (jewelry, ties, belts, hats), mannequin, hangers, mirrors

Pet Store:
stuffed animals, live animals (ones that live in cages), instructions for pet care, pet food, feeding dishes, pet toys

Grocery Store:
empty food containers and cans, "fake" fruits and vegetables (or laminate large cutouts from newpapers and magazines), scale or balance, aprons for clerks, coupons (real or patterns on page 11)

Garden Shop:
flowers (real or artificial), small house plants, pots and vases, potting soil, seed packets, watering can

Toy Store:
trucks and cars, stuffed animals, balls, games, action figures

Bookstore:
bookmarks, greeting cards

Art Gallery:
student art, price tags, easels, guest book

Checklist of Skills ✔

Students' Names

Skills									
Reads environmental print.									
Matches samples of environmental print that are the same.									
Matches words that are the same in different environmental print samples.									
Uses print in dramatic play.									
Identifies objects that fit into a specific category.									
Recognizes own name in print.									
Recognizes classmates' names in print.									
Follows print in book as book is read.									
Reads familiar words in context.									
Puts events of a story or situation in order.									
Puts known words together to make a familiar sentence.									
Dictates a message.									
Writes a message.									
Shows enthusiasm for reading.									
Shows enthusiasm for writing.									

Price Tags

Here is the price:

Here is the price:

Here is the price:

Here is the price:

Here is the price:

Here is the price:

Here is the price:

Here is the price:

Here is the price:

Reading While You Shop EMC 565

Store Receipts

Receipt of Purchase

Date: _____

Amount: _____

Receipt of Purchase

Date: _____

Amount: _____

Receipt of Purchase

Date: _____

Amount: _____

Receipt of Purchase

Date: _____

Amount: _____

Name Tags

May I help you?

My name is

_____

- - - - - - - - - - - - - - -

_____

May I help you?

My name is

_____

- - - - - - - - - - - - - - -

_____

May I help you?

My name is

_____

- - - - - - - - - - - - - - -

_____

May I help you?

My name is

_____

- - - - - - - - - - - - - - -

_____

Come in...

We're Open

Closed

Please come back again!

Our Store

Shoppers' Coupon

Save 50 Cents on
paper plates

Superstrong

Shoppers' Coupon

Cool beans
Cool taste

Save 25 cents
when you buy
JELLYBEANS

Shoppers' Coupon

Buy One • Get one FREE

Save $1

Shoppers' Coupon

Save 30 cents
on any mustard

Shoppers' Coupon

Save 20 cents
on a loaf of bread

Shoppers' Coupon

Potato Chips
2 bags for $1

Shoppers' Coupon

Fruit Punch
3 for $1

SAVE 50 cents

Shoppers' Coupon

Pasta-O's
50 cents

SAVE 27 cents

Learning About Shopping

What Is Shopping?

1. Have students tell what shopping means. Write their ideas on a large piece of chart paper. Discuss differences and similarities of ideas. Locate common ideas and write a class definition of shopping. Record that definition on a chart that you post.

2. Read Rosemary Wells' account of a shopping trip in **Max's Dragon Shirt** (Dial Books, 1991). Ask each student to describe shopping experiences he/she has had. Write each description on a blank page and have the child illustrate it. Combine the pages to make a class book.

Shopping
We spend money to buy things we need.
food
clothes
books

Where Do You Shop?

Brainstorm a list of the stores where your students shop. Write each location on a large card. Use the cards in the following activities:

1. Show one card and read the name of the shop. Discuss what types of things would be found in the shop. Have a student draw pictures on the card to show some of the things named. Post the illustrated cards to create a word bank of store names.

SHOE STORE
DRUG STORE
BOOK STORE
SUPERMARKET

2. Label several small boxes with the store names. Reproduce the picture cards on pages 13-16. Have students match each picture card to a store that would sell that product. Note: some items could be sold in more than one type of store.

BIKE STORE

PET STORE

loaf of bread

bagel

buns

cookies

cake

French bread loaf

sandals

high-top tennis shoes

mary janes

bedroom slippers

hiking boots

snow boots

goldfish

dog food

hamster cage

collar and leash

canary

water and food dish for cat

KITTY

KITTY

ball

doll

stuffed animal

truck

bike

puzzle

Reading While You Shop EMC 565

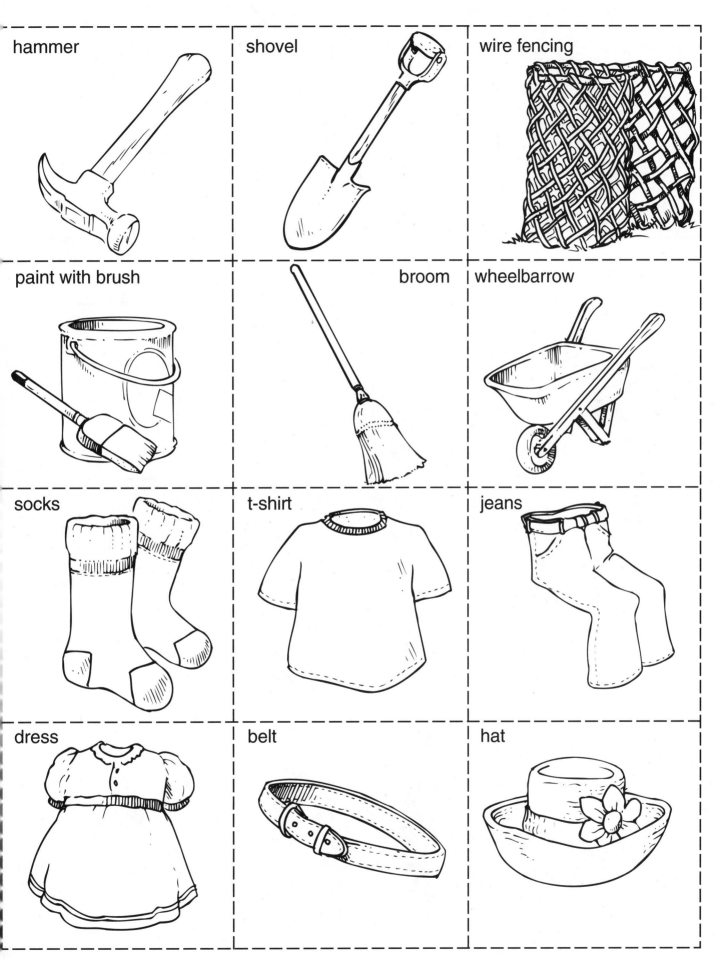

hammer

shovel

wire fencing

paint with brush

broom

wheelbarrow

socks

t-shirt

jeans

dress

belt

hat

can of tuna

frozen pizza

box of detergent

PIZZA

CLEAN!

pretzel

carton of orange juice

ORANGE JUICE

sack of potatoes

POTATOES

tricycle

bike pump

bike helmet

skateboard

bicycle wheel

water bottle

Water

Shopping Lists

My Shopping List

Copy the poem, *My Shopping List* (page 1), on a large chart or make a transparency to use on the overhead projector.

- Read the poem to your class. Have students identify the items that the shopper is looking for. Circle the words that name the items in the poem. Have students tell which stores would have the items that are circled.

- Cover circled words with sticky notes. Reproduce the word cards on page 18 and distribute them to students. Read the poem again. Have students bring up the word card that matches the word that fits in each covered space.

Writing a Shopping List in the Classroom

1. Reproduce the picture cards on pages 13-16. Display them in your classroom. (You may wish to enlarge them.)
2. Reproduce a copy of *My Shopping List* on page 19 for each student. Have them choose three to five things to write on the list.
3. Students then exchange shopping lists, read their new lists, and "shop" for picture cards.

Writing a Shopping List

Have students work in pairs to write a shopping list for a specific event. Young students can draw items on the list. Label the pictures as the students read their picture lists back to you.

Shopping lists might be created for:
- a birthday party
- a picnic
- making a bird house

Shopping Lists at Home

Reproduce the parent letter on page 20. Send the letter home and have students go shopping with their families. A family member will write a shopping list and then accompany the student on a shopping trip to buy the items on the list.

When signed lists are returned to school, record each **Super Shopper's** name on a special poster.

My Shopping List

My Shopping List

Reading While You Shop EMC 565

Dear Parent,

We have been practicing our reading skills by reading and writing shopping lists. The next time you go to the store with your child, please use this form to write a list of 3-5 items that the child can find. Let your child lead the way, reading the environmental print, and locating the items. When the shopping is done, sign the list, and return it to school. We will keep track of our Super Shoppers!

Thank you.

Sincerely,

My Shopping List

1. _____

2. _____

3. _____

4. _____

5. _____

_____
Parent Signature

                   Reading While You Shop EMC 565

Field Trips

Shopping field trips provide wonderful opportunities for practicing reading. Do the following activities with your class to prepare for shopping field trips.

1. Prepare a list of the items you want to buy. Try to make this an authentic shopping trip by purchasing something that your class actually needs: supplies for the class pet, a new game or book, or the ingredients for a cooking project. Practice reading the words on the list so that your students will be able to locate the items at the store.

2. Have your students compose a group letter to parents explaining the shopping trip and recruiting helpers to accompany the class. Reproduce the letter and have students add their personal messages and drawings to the notes before sending them home.

3. Trace the route of your trip on a map of your community. Discuss which stores would carry the items that you are looking for. Find the best route for getting to those stores.

After the trip, follow up with these activities:

1. Reproduce the shopping journal form on page 22. Have students draw, write, or dictate an account of the trip. They should describe how they located their items. Record an account of each shopping trip that your class makes and combine them in a class *Shopping Journal*.

2. Write thank you notes to the merchants whose stores you visited.

Note: If lines are desired, insert your writing paper before reproducing.

We Went Shopping

Reading While You Shop EMC 565

Note: Read this poem with your students and discuss window shopping. Using the reproducible on page 24, have each student draw what they would like to see in a store window.

Window Shopping

We went looking, my mom and I,

To see the latest styles.

We looked at all the mannequins.

We walked and walked for miles.

We moved quickly from store to store.

We didn't miss a single one.

Our feet were tired, our heads were full

When our looking trip was done.

Jill Norris

Note: Reproduce this page to use with the poem, *Window Shopping* (page 23).

I Saw It in the Window

Draw what you would like to see in a store's window.

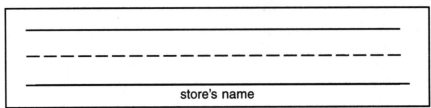

store's name

Reading Environmental Print

As you shop, you are surrounded by print. The print is on commercial signs, billboards, labels, and logos. This is called environmental print. Young students recognize it, not so much because of the letters or words, but because of the colors, pictures, and shapes that surround the print. Often environmental print is the first print that a child recognizes.

Use the environmental print activities provided in this section throughout your shopping unit. Choose those activities that are appropriate to your students.

When you are working with environmental print, remember:
- The environmental print that a child recognizes depends on the child's life experiences.
- Environmental print should be used in full context, if possible. The colors, pictures, and shapes that surround the letters and words are all important context.

Collecting Samples

Ask your students to start collecting samples of environmental print to bring to school.
- Copy the parent letter on page 26 and send it home with students.
- Provide a large manila envelope, a folder, or a bag to store each student's samples.
- Use the samples for the reading readiness activities that follow (pages 27-32).

Dear Parents,

Shopping is an activity common to every family. Have you ever considered how much reading you do as you shop? In class we are talking about this type of reading. The labels on the cereal and peanut butter, the logo on a favorite fast-food restaurant, and the stop sign at the corner are called environmental print. The colors, pictures, and shapes that surround the print help us to recognize and read it.

Environmental print may be the first print that children recognize. Then they move on to reading the words, first without the color and then without the pictures and shapes that surround them. Recognizing environmental print is an important first step in reading and makes students feel successful.

As you shop, encourage your child to read environmental print. Read the labels of food items. When you run errands, read traffic signs and billboards. In the store, read signs and labels on the products.

We are starting a collection of environmental print for our classroom. Please collect familiar print samples with your child. Newspaper and magazine ads are an excellent source for print samples, as well as coupons and labels on packaged foods. Send in as many samples as you can; repeats are welcome. These samples will be used for various activities, including puzzles, games, and scrapbooks.

Start collecting today. Thank you.

Sincerely,

Making Environmental Print Books

Plastic sleeves that fit in a three-ring binder make great pages for environmental print books. Samples can be placed in the sleeves and then removed for activities. Or, environmental print samples can be mounted on construction paper pages and stapled into books.

Three Different Books

Category Books

Organize the samples of print in books such as Our Favorite Foods, Favorite Places to Eat, Signs We See. Be sure to discuss why samples are included in a particular book. Some samples may fit in more than one category.

A Class ABC Book

Arrange the print samples in an ABC book. Provide a page for each letter and attach samples to the pages. Note that some letters have more samples than others.

Individual Books

As students bring in their samples of environmental print, mount the samples in an I Can Read book. Allow time for reading and sharing books . Encourage students to match samples that are alike or to identify matching words in different samples.

Using the Books

- Put the books in centers for students to share and enjoy.
- Choose a *Reader for the Day* to read the scrapbook at circle time.
- Ask all students to look through their own books to identify a specific product that would fit in a category you name: cereals, fast foods, etc.
- Include books in assessment portfolios.

Games Using Environmental Print

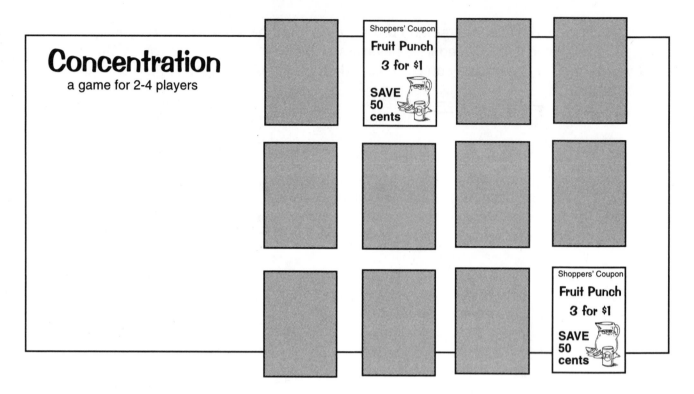

Concentration
a game for 2-4 players

Materials:
- rectangles of tag board (Adjust the size to fit the size of your print samples.)
- 5-10 pairs of matching print samples
- glue

Preparation:

1. Cut rectangles of tag board to an equal size.

2. Mount 5-10 matching pairs of print samples on the tag board rectangles.

3. Laminate the cards for durability.

How to play:

1. Place all the cards, sample side down, on a playing surface.

2. The first player turns over two cards and reads the samples, trying to find a matching pair. If the two samples match, the player keeps the pair and takes another turn. If the samples do not match, the cards are turned back over and a new player takes a turn.

3. When all cards have been matched, the player with the most pairs is the winner.

Puzzles

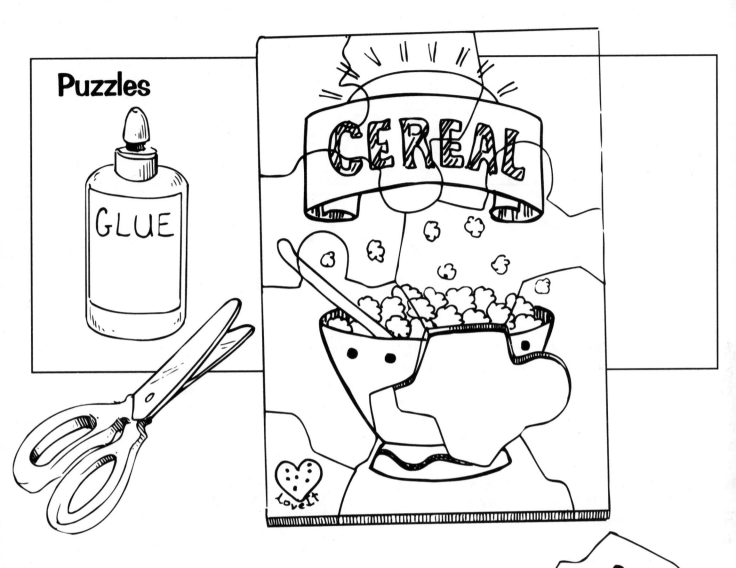

Making the puzzles:

1. Remove the front of a prepared food box. (Cereal boxes, cake mix boxes, and pudding boxes work well.)

2. Cut the box front into puzzle pieces.

3. Store the pieces in a duplicate box. The storage box can be used as a guide for assembling the puzzle.

Using the puzzles:

Encourage students to read the puzzle after they put it together.

Print Lotto

Materials:
- 1 lotto board (page 31) per player
- nine 2" square (5 cm) tag board squares per player
- duplicate samples of environmental print from magazines, newpapers, product labels, etc. One sample will be used for the lotto board and one for the playing card.
- glue

Preparation:
1. Glue one print sample into each square of the lotto boards. **Every square on every board** will have a different print sample.

2. Glue duplicate print samples to the small tag board squares.

3. Laminate for durability.

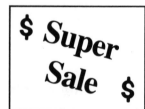

How to play:
1. Give each player a lotto board. Put all lotto cards face down in the center of the playing area.

2. One student turns over a playing card and reads the print. The student having that sample on the lotto board gets the card and lays it on top of the matching space. If no one claims the sample, the card goes onto a discard pile.

3. Students take turns flipping the playing cards and reading them. The first player to cover his/her game board wins.

         Reading While You Shop EMC 565

Print Lotto

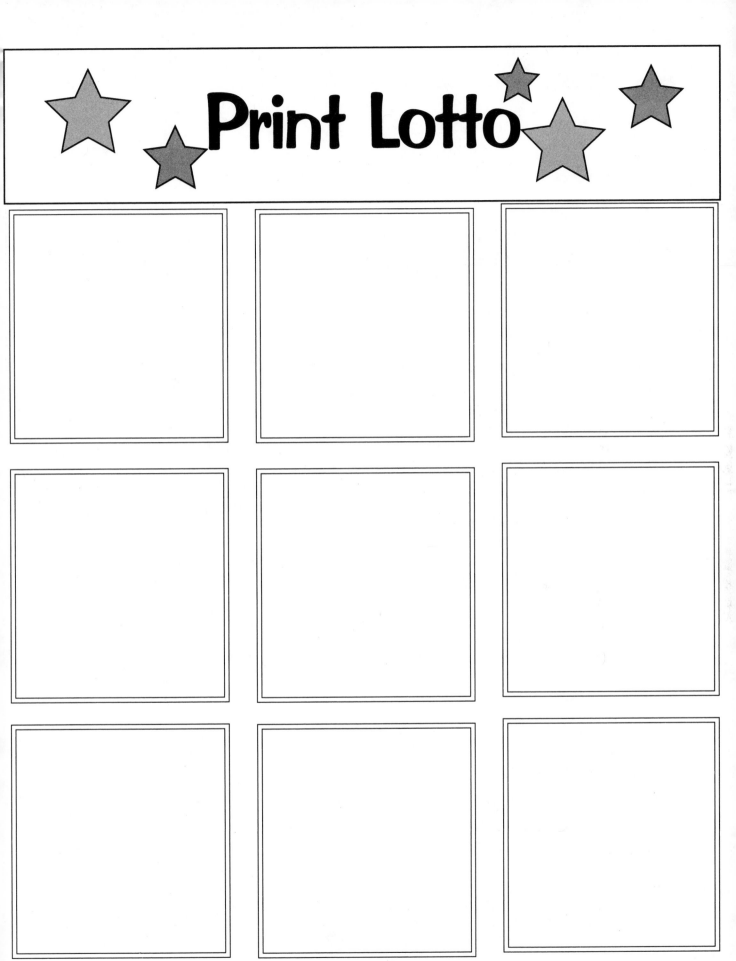

Reading While You Shop EMC 565

A Shopping Trip Board Game

Materials:
- shopping game board
- numbered cube or die
- game pieces

Preparation:

1. On a large piece of tag or poster board, create a game board such as the one at right.

2. Personalize the empty squares of the playing board by gluing small samples of environmental print to the board before laminating it. Small samples are often found in magazine advertisements or on coupons.

3. Reproduce the game pieces below. Fold and glue them so that they stand by themselves.

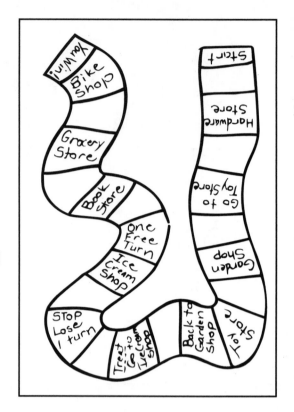

How to play:

1. Each player rolls the cube and moves a playing piece along the path, in turn.
2. Players read the print samples and directions as they move. Encourage students to help each other read the print.
3. The first person to get home is the winner.

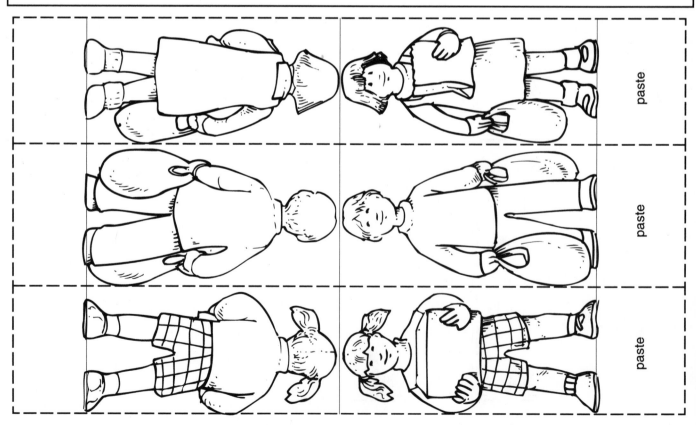

Shoppers' Activity Pages

Let's go shopping,
you and I.
What do you think
that we should buy?

The reproducible activities on pages 35-46 are identified by this logo. Pages 34 and 38 are teacher pages.

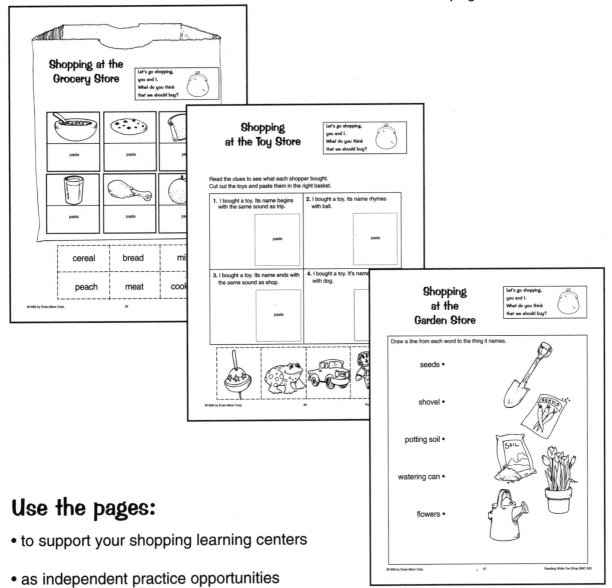

Use the pages:

• to support your shopping learning centers

• as independent practice opportunities

• as a starting point for a lesson on a specific readiness skill

• to make a shopper's reading manual

Reading While You Shop EMC 565

The Grocery Store

1. Read the poem *The Grocery Store* to your class.

2. As you read the poem, have students act it out using real props.

3. Have students write the list that the person in the poem might have carried. (Reproduce page 19.)

4. Identify rhyming words in the poem as you read it another time.

5. Reproduce page 35. Have students cut out the words and match them with the pictures in the grocery bag.

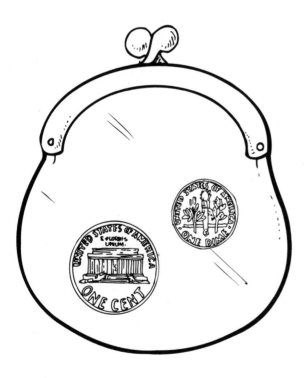

The Grocery Store

I made a list.
I read it through.
I knew just what
I had to do.

Cereal first,
Bread, milk, and tea.
I'll choose a peach
Just right for me.

Next the noodles,
the sauce, the meat.
I bet you'll guess
What I will eat.

I can't resist
The cookie row.
I'll grab a few
Before I go.

I go up front
So I can pay.
My shopping's done
For another day.

Jill Norris

Shopping at the Grocery Store

Let's go shopping,
you and I.
What do you think
that we should buy?

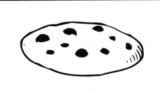

paste

paste

paste

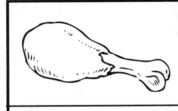

paste

paste

paste

cereal	bread	milk
peach	meat	cookies

Reading While You Shop EMC 565

Shopping at the Toy Store

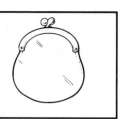

Read the clues to see what each shopper bought.
Cut out the toys and paste them in the right basket.

1. I bought a toy. Its name ends with the same sound as shop.

paste

2. I bought a toy. Its name rhymes with ball.

paste

3. I bought a toy. Its name begins with the same sound as trip.

paste

4. I bought a toy. Its name rhymes with dog.

paste

Shopping at the Garden Store

Draw a line from each word to the thing it names.

seeds •

shovel •

potting soil •

watering can •

flowers •

Reading While You Shop EMC 565

Shopping
at the Clothing Store

1. Sing this song to the traditional tune: *Mary Wore a Red Dress*.

Mary bought a red dress,

red dress,

red dress.

Mary bought a red dress at the store.

Tommy bought a green shirt,

green shirt,

green shirt,

Tommy bought a green shirt at the store.

Alex bought a brown hat,

brown hat,

brown hat.

Alex bought a brown hat at the store.

Ashley bought a yellow belt,

yellow belt,

yellow belt.

Ashley bought a yellow belt at the store.

2. Reproduce page 39 for each student to practice reading color words.

 Reading While You Shop EMC 565

Mary Bought a
Red Dress

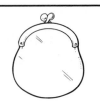

red   brown   yellow   green

I would buy a _____ _____.

1. Read the signs.
2. Look at the clothes.
3. Put the signs on the right displays.

Shopping at the Clothing Store

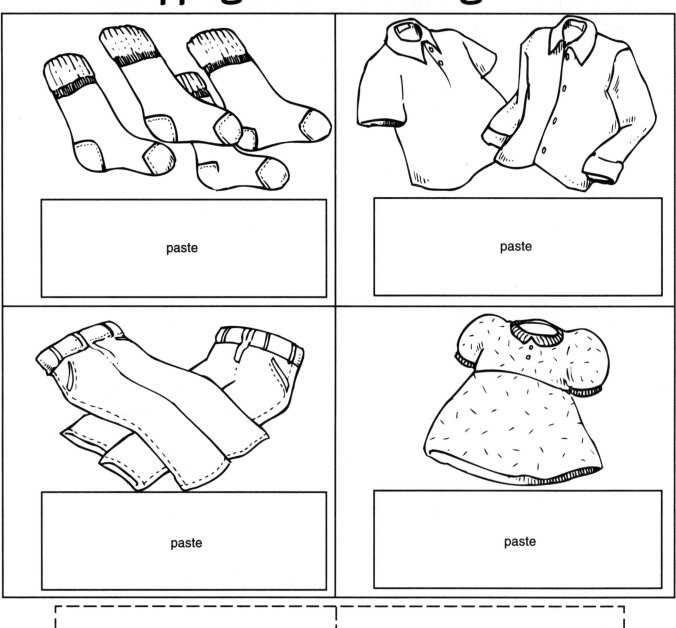

paste

paste

paste

paste

Socks for Sale

Buy a Dress

Shirts   **$10.00**

Pants
Buy One, Get One Free

Shopping at the Bike Shop

Help Pat find the things on her shopping list.
Write the words with the pictures.

| helmet | lock | bike | bell |

Pat's Shopping List

Shopping at the Bookstore

Give each book the correct title.

paste

paste

paste

paste

The Little Red Hen

Trucks Work for Us

Three Funny Monkeys

How to Make a Birdhouse

42

Reading While You Shop EMC 56

Shopping at the Video Store

The tapes at the Video Store are kept in ABC order.
Put the new tapes where they belong.

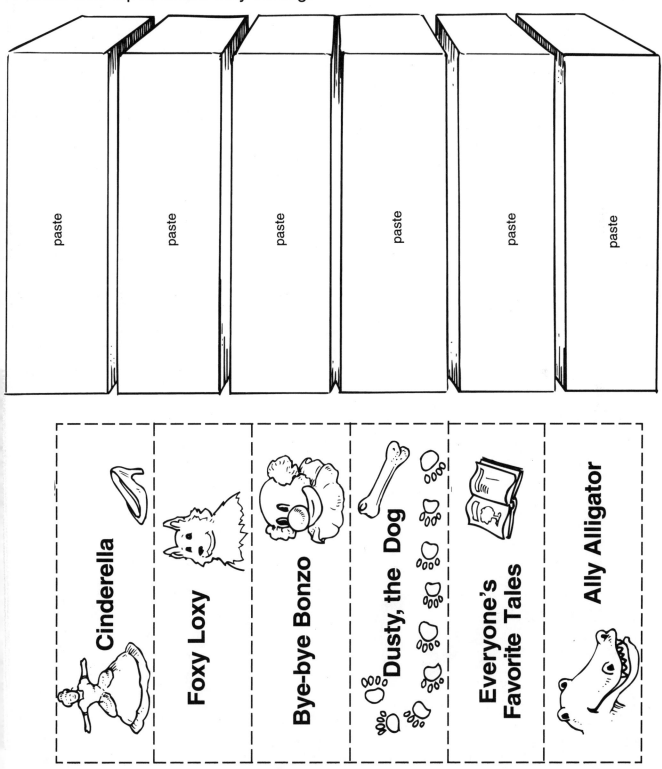

paste   paste   paste   paste   paste   paste

Cinderella

Foxy Loxy

Bye-bye Bonzo

Dusty, the Dog

Everyone's Favorite Tales

Ally Alligator

Shopping at the Shoe Store

Match the shoes to the shoppers.

I want mary janes, size 9, please.

paste

I want boots, please.

paste

I want high-tops, please.

paste

I want sandals, size 6, please.

paste

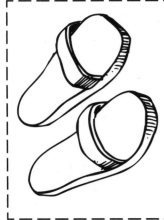

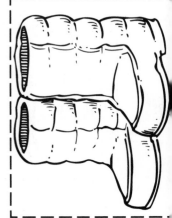

Shopping at the Furniture Store

Let's go shopping,
you and I.
What do you think
that we should buy?

The sign lost some words. Choose words from the word bank below. Fill in the blanks so that the sign makes sense.

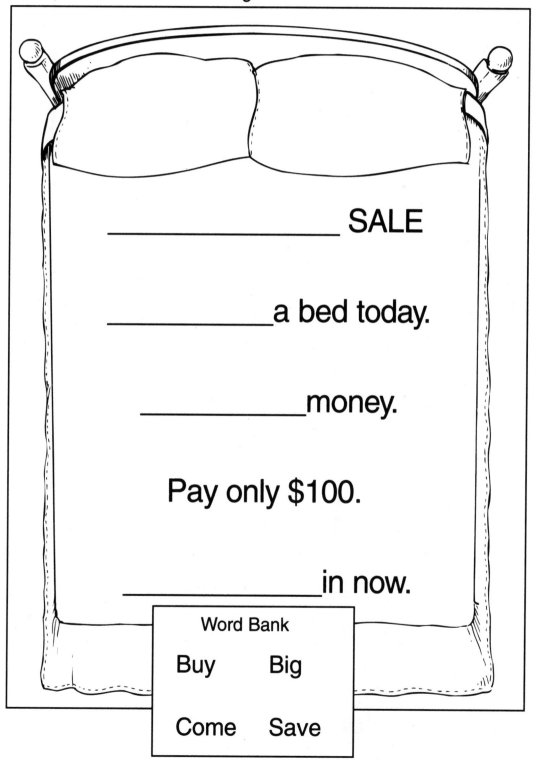

_____ SALE

_____a bed today.

_____money.

Pay only $100.

_____in now.

Word Bank

Buy	Big
Come	Save

Shopping at the Flower Shop

Read the labels.
Follow the directions to color the flowers.

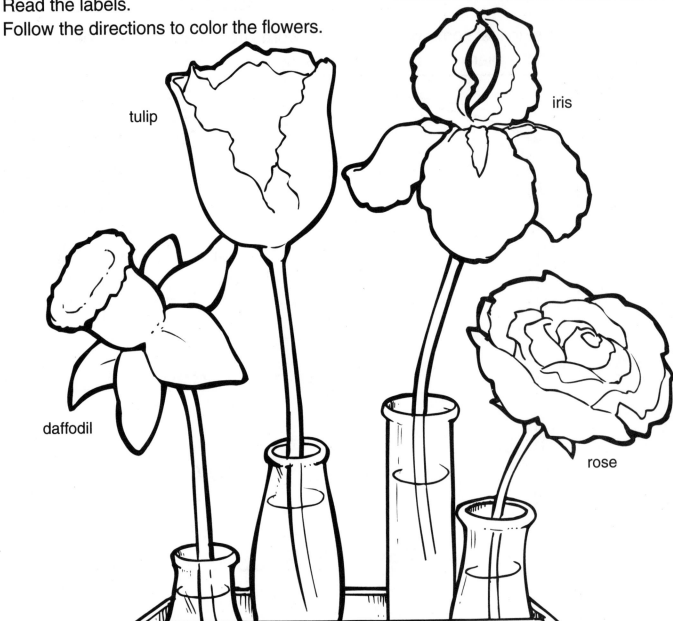

tulip

iris

daffodil

rose

Color the daffodil yellow.

Color the iris blue.

Color the rose pink.

Color the tulip purple.

Reproducible
Beginning Readers

Teaching Ideas

Reproducible pages are provided for two minibooks:
• *What Did You Buy?* (pages 56-58)
• *Shop* (pages 59-63)

Making Each Book

1. Reproduce the beginning reader for each student.

2. Cut the pages in half and staple them in order to form a little book.

3. Put a piece of construction paper or plastic tape over the staples to form the bindings.

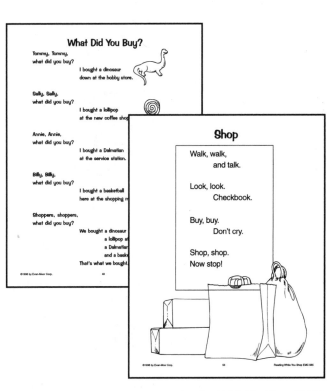

How to Use Both Books

1. Read the story to the class.

2. Distribute individual booklets and reread the story with students following along.

3. Make a transparency of the story text:
   • Page 49 - *What Did You Buy?*
   • Page 53 - *Shop*

4. Project an enlarged copy using an overhead projector.
   Encourage students to:
   • find words that are alike in the the text
   • identify words that they know
   • identify a word you cover up by using context clues

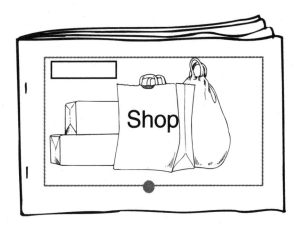

5. Copy each line of the text onto sentence strips. Distribute the strips to students.
- Read the story and have students stand when the line on their strip is read.
- Have students hold their strips and arrange themselves in story order. Read the story off the strips to check the order.

> *Tommy, Tommy, what did you buy?*

6. Have students work with individual words in the text.
Word cards for ***What Did You Buy?*** are on pages 50-51.
Word cards for ***Shop*** are on page 54.

That's what we bought.

That's   what   we   bought

- Reproduce the word cards.
- Cut the word cards apart.
- Have students choose the word cards to match specific words that you name.
- Have students use the word cards to make a given line of the story.

7. Have students write and draw to complete the reproducible activity sheet that accompanies each book.

> ***What Did You Buy***, page 52:
> - students fill their names in the blanks on the top of their pages
> - students write or dictate the name of their purchase and where they bought it
>   Note: student lines do not need to rhyme
> - students then draw a picture of what they "bought"

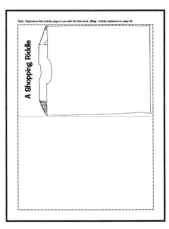

> ***Shop***, page 55:
> - students cut out the pattern and fold on the fold line
> - students draw something inside the folder
> - students write or dictate a riddle about the item
> - paste the riddles on the outside of the bag
> - classmates try to guess the answers to each other's riddles

What Did You Buy?

Tommy, Tommy,
what did you buy?

I bought a dinosaur
down at the hobby store.

Sally, Sally,
what did you buy?

I bought a lollipop
at the new coffee shop.

Annie, Annie,
what did you buy?

I bought a Dalmatian
at the service station.

Billy, Billy,
what did you buy?

I bought a basketball
here at the shopping mall.

Shoppers, shoppers,
what did you buy?

We bought a dinosaur at the hobby store,
a lollipop at the coffee shop,
a Dalmatian at the service station,
and a basketball at the shopping mall.
That's what we bought.

Reading While You Shop EMC 565

buy	dinosaur	hobby store	coffee shop
you	a	the	new
did	bought	at	lollipop
what	I	down	Sally

? .	That's	shopping mall	Tommy
We	service station	here	and
Shoppers	Dalmatian	basketball	we
here	Annie	Billy	Shoppers

_____

– – – – – – – – – – – – – – – – – – –

_____ '

name

_____

– – – – – – – – – – – – – – – – – – –

_____

name

What did you buy?

_____

– – – – – – – – – – – – – – – – – – – –

I bought a _____

_____

– – – – – – – – – – – – – – – – – – – –

at the _____

Shop

Walk, walk,
    and talk.

Look, look.
    Checkbook.

Buy, buy.
    Don't cry.

Shop, shop.
    Now stop!

Note: Reproduce these word cards to use with the little book, *Shop.* (See page 48.)

talk.	stop!	cry.
and	Now	Don't	Checkbook.
walk,	shop.	buy.	look.
Walk,	Shop,	Buy,	Look,

A Shopping Riddle

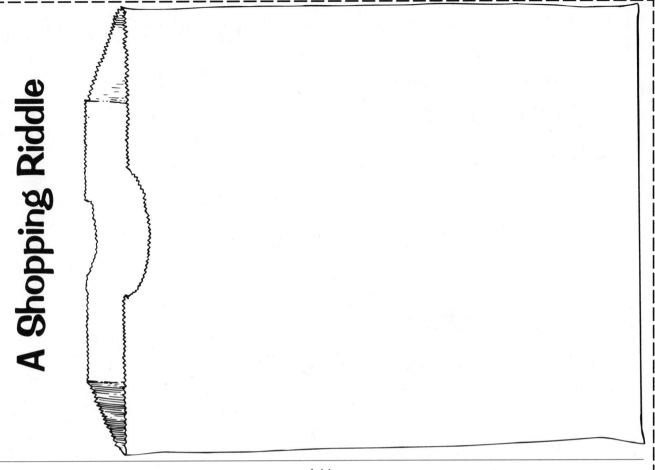

fold

My Book

Name_____

Tommy, Tommy,
what did you buy?

I bought a dinosaur
down at the hobby store.

1

Sally, Sally,
what did you buy?

I bought a lollipop
at the new coffee shop.

2

Annie, Annie,
what did you buy?

I bought a Dalmatian
at the service station.

3

Billy, Billy,
what did you buy?

I bought a basketball
here at the shopping mall.

4

Shoppers, shoppers,
what did you buy?

We bought a dinosaur at the grocery store,

a lollipop at the coffee shop,

a Dalmatian at the service station,

and a basketball at the shopping mall.

5

That's what we bought.

6

Shop

1

Walk, walk,

2

and talk.

3

Look, look.

4

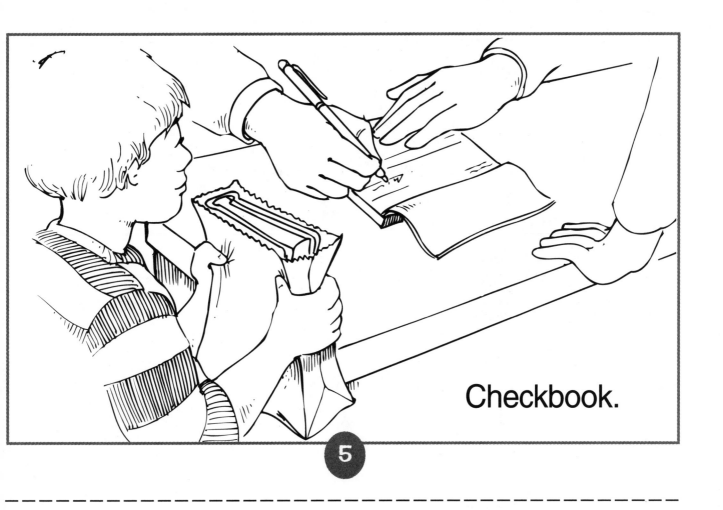

Checkbook.

5

Buy, buy.

6

Don't cry.

7

Shop,

8

shop.

Now stop!

_____

_ _

_____
name

You are a Super Shopper.

You can read the words around you as you shop.

Congratulations!

from _____